BEGINNING BLUES GUITAR

AN INSTRUCTION MANUAL BY JERRY SILVERMAN

Oak Publications
New York/London/Sydney

Well, the blues...I always just called plain old bein' lonesome. Now, a lot of people don't think that that's a big enough word—but then, you can get lonesome for a lot of things. People down from where I come from, they're lonesome for a job, they're lonesome for some spendin' money, lonesome for some drinkin' whiskey, lonesome for good times, pretty gals—wine, women and song like they see stuck up in their face every day by other people. Thinkin' maybe that you're down and out—disgusted and busted and can't be trusted. Gives you a lonesome feeling that somehow the world's sorta turned against you or there's somethin' about it you don't understand. Bein' out of work. Bein' lonesome.

Woody Guthrie

Documentary and news photographs by David Gahr
Photographic selection and layout by Moses Asch
Cover photograph of Robert Pete Williams by Herb Wise

Copyright © 1964 by Oak Publications,
A Division of Music Sales Corporation, New York, NY.

Order No. OK 63461
International Standard Book Number: 0.8256.0009.X
Library of Congress Catalog Card Number: 64-18168

Exclusive Distributors:
Music Sales Corporation
257 Park Avenue South, New York, NY 10010 USA
Music Sales Limited
8/9 Frith Street, London W1V 5TZ England
Music Sales Pty. Limited
120 Rothschild Street, Rosebery, Sydney, NSW 2018, Australia

Printed in the United States of America by
Vicks Lithograph and Printing Corporation

CONTENTS

A beginning blues book is not a beginning guitar book. The student will be assumed to have at least a general familiarity with folk guitar basics - tuning the instrument, common chords in the keys of C, G, D, A and E major, some barre chord positions (not absolutely necessary, but helpful), some facility with the right hand (particularly arpeggios). If you feel shaky on any of these points you would do well to refer to a prior publication, The Folksinger's Guitar Guide by Silverman and Seeger, (Oak Publications).

INTRODUCTION

Of all the areas of folk guitar technique in America it is the in the realm of the blues guitar that the most possibilities are offered for the creative and imaginative guitarist. Conversely, if one calls to mind names of outstanding folk guitarists (not necessarily popular folk singers who also strum along) the chances are that 99% of them will have made their mark in the world of blues.

Through the years of teaching folk guitar it has been made abundantly clear to me by countless students that after the first level of competance has been achieved (basic chords, "strums", and a general ease with the instrument) that it is a desire to play (and sing) blues - among other things, of course - that motivates further study, As in all folk-musical endeavors merely "taking lessons" never suffices, but particularly in the introspective, highly personalized and technically advanced world of the blues guitar is it necessary to engage in extensive and intensive listening, watching and imitating.

Naturally, some basis of what to listen and watch for and whom to imitate must be laid. Throwing the fledgling bluesnik into the turbulent waters of Bluesville without the necessary basic information and technique would render a distinct disservice to the general cause- not to mention the specific aspirant.

A student of mine who received her education- general and musical- in Europe once put this question to me:

"Most of the folk songs I know from central Europe bear a general similarity to each other. But for the language differences a German folk song might be a French one or a Danish or an English... But here in America I hear an altogether different kind of folk music. Why is this? What is the reason for this different feeling...?"

The answer, although obvious, was one that I had never particularly thought of before in quite those terms: The tremendous influence of African culture through the Negro in America.

My perceptive European-born student detected this influence without specifically being able to identify it. Through her questions I began, myself, to take a new look at old friends - Negro-American music and "musicianers".

The debt of American popular music to blues being well known as well as the continuing interest of folk guitarists in the blues genre one might assume that there would be an extensive literature on the subject.

Not so!

The fact of the matter is that there is more information on blues in general in the New York Public Library, for example, in German and French than there is in English!

I first came across this startling bit of intelligence when using (or rather, attempting to use) the Library's files while doing the preliminary research on my Master's Thesis ("The Blues Guitar As Illustrated by the Practices of Blind Lemon Jefferson, Huddie Ledbetter (Leadbelly) and Josh White", New York University, 1955).

It was this glaring lack of documentation on what may properly be called our "national musical heritage" that delivered the primary impetus toward the compilation and publication of my first book, "Folk Blues" (Macmillan, 1958 - Oak paperback, 1964). This volume brought together for the first time under one cover a hopefully representative collection of (110) folk blues. "Folk Blues" contains piano arrangements of the songs as well as the customary chord symbols. It was felt that bona fide guitar arrangements would limit the book's general usefullness. However, many guitaristic passages were integrated into the piano part and those desiring to explore them were and are urged to do so.

Nevertheless, the basic question of "how do you play the blues" was left largely unanswered. To the extent that any "answer" is possible this book will attempt to fill in some of the blanks. We will start with relatively simple blues patterns and rhythms and develop gradually into complicated solo and accompaniment passages. Some transcriptions of recorded performances will be presented as well as a great deal of original material.

Oh, yes, there is one other point that would bear mentioning here: What is blues?

Well, it's a good question.

In it's most basic form a folk blues has
a three line stanza,
a characteristic melody (often twelve measures long), and three or four simple chords.

In its most refined form it is a free rhythmic, melodic, harmonic and lyric expression a particular performer's innermost feelings at one specific time - that time coinciding with the actual performance.

Let your own definition grow out of your own experience and the pages of this book...

THE RIGHT KIND OF GUITAR

Whereas in general folk guitaring there may be a difference of opinion as to the relative merits and uses of steel-string guitars versus nylon-string guitars, in the world of the blues guitar there can be no doubt which instrument is the "right" one. All - let me repeat for emphasis - _all_ the guitarists who are considered blues instrumentalists play steel-string instruments!

While one may play a blues on a nylon strung guitar, many of the specific techniques (such as choking and playing with a pick) become well-nigh meaningless and the general sound, so characteristic of the real blues guitar, just doesn't come through at all.

If you already have a nylon instrument you can begin to work on this book but sooner or later you'll have to switch over. When you do, do yourself a favor and get a good instrument. A good steel-string guitar with low, sensitive action can be a joy to play and a revelation to those of you to whom the words "steel strings" conjure up images of bloody, blistered fingers.

TABLATURE
MELTAB and GITAB

Ever since the invention of music notation countless generations of instrumentalists have been trying to avoid learning to read music. During the last 700 years or so elaborate systems have been developed to show the player which holes to cover, which key to press, which string to pluck or which fret to stop, instead of the actual note on the musical staff. These systems are referred to generally as "tablature".

The general desire to avoid learning to read music is nowhere more prevalent than among "folk" instrumentalists and singers. They consider · perhaps rightly so - the printed music page to be an intrusion upon a highly personal art form. A form whose greatest practitioners have not been fettered by pieces of paper. A form where creation and performance often took place in the same breath - a breath that was often labored due to the swinging of a sledge hammer, the pulling of a rope or the lifting of a bale.

If in the very act of writing such a book as this we do violence to this sacred tradition it is only in an effort to preserve it. But then we are squarely faced with a circular paradox: How can you teach music without, in fact, teaching _music_?

In this best of all possible worlds it is possible to work one's way out of all dilemmas. What we shall do is combine standard music notation for the melody of the song with its tablature ("MELTAB") and standard musical notation for the guitar with its tablature ("GITAB") as follows:

The spaces above each of the six lines indicate the strings of the guitar.

1st String - E
2nd String - B
3rd String - G
4th String - D
5th String - A
6th String - E

The numbers in each space indicate at what fret the string is pressed to the fingerboard by a finger of the left hand. Thus, if you played a scale starting on the lowest string

tablature would show it in this manner:

MELTAB when used will be written directly below the melody line. GITAB when used will be written directly below the guitar part.

By the use of MELTAB it will be possible for the student to play the melody of all the songs in the book. In addition to being able to learn the tunes thereby, playing the melody is a vital factor in blues guitar performance. This will be gone into in some detail throughout the body of this book.

GITAB (and the guitar part itself) will be written out only when there is a specific need to illustrate some point. Experience has shown that is unnecessary and confusing to write out measure after measure of a repetitive strum when merely describing it once would suffice.

BASIC BLUES ARPEGGIO

"Oh, it don't mean a thing if it ain't got that swing. "

Do you remember that song? I think that was the only lyric it had and a truer sentiment was never expressed. "That swing" can be gotten on the guitar in a variety of ways. The basic rhythmic feeling, or swing, in blues is a series of long-short, long-short alternating beats. Like a series of dashes and dots: — · — · — · A poet would call this meter, "trochaic".

If you're not sure what this means try intoning "The Raven" schoolboy fashion accenting the underlined syllables:

<u>Once</u> upon a <u>mid</u>night <u>drea</u>ry
As I <u>pon</u>dered <u>weak</u> and <u>wea</u>ry
<u>O</u>ver <u>man</u>y a <u>quaint</u> and <u>cur</u>ious
<u>Vol</u>ume <u>of</u> for<u>got</u>ten <u>lore</u>...

In musical notation the rhythm would look like this:

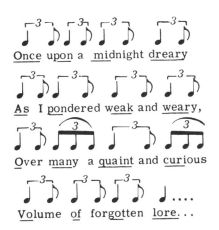

Once upon a midnight dreary

As I pondered weak and weary,

Over many a quaint and curious

Volume of forgotten lore...

This trochaic (or triplet) rhythm may be played in a variety of ways.

Let's try a simple arpeggio involving the thumb, first, second and third fingers together, and the first finger again:

thumb   1   2   1   thumb   1   2   1
                   3   3

Try the same thing with different chords. Make sure all the strings sound clearly.

A good song that we all know which has this rhythm pretty much all the way through is "Frankie and Johnny".

8

Frankie and Johnny went walking,
Johnny in his brand-new suit.
"Oh, Good Lord", said Frankie,
"Don't my Johnny man look cute?"
He was her man, but he done her wrong.

Johnny said, "I've got to leave you,
"But I won't be very long.
"Don't wait up for me, honey,
"Or worry while I'm gone,"
He was her man...

Frankie went down to the corner,
Went in the saloon for some beer.
She said to the fat bartender,
"Has my Johnny man been here?"
He was her man...

"Well, I ain't gonna tell you no story,
"And I ain't gonna tell you no lie.
"I saw your Johnny 'bout an hour ago
"With a gal named Nellie Bly.
"If he's your man, he's a-doin' you wrong".

Frankie got off at South 12th Street,
She didn't go there for fun,
For under her long red kimono
She carried a forty-four gun.
He was her man...

Frankie went into the hotel,
Looked up in the window so high.
There she saw her Johnny
A-lovin' up Nellie Bly.
He was her man...

Johnny saw Frankie a-comin',
Down the backstairs he did scoot.
Frankie pulled out her pistol
And the gun went rooty-toot-toot.
He was her man, but she shot him down.

"Roll me over so easy,
"Roll me over so slow.
"Roll me over on my right side,
"For my left side hurts me so.
"I was her man, but I done her wrong."

Bring out your rubber-tired hearses,
Bring out your old-time hack.
Twelve men going to the graveyard
And eleven coming back.
He was her man...

Now it was not murder in the second degree,
And it was not murder in the third.
That woman simply dropped her man
Like a hunter drops a bird.
He was her man...

"Oh, bring out a thousand policemen,
"Lock me into your cell,
"For I've shot my Johnny so dead
"I know I'm going to hell.
"He was my man, but I shot him down."

Frankie mounted to the scaffold
As calm as a girl could be,
And turning her eyes to heaven
She said, "Nearer, my God, to Thee".
He was her man...

Notice all the musical activity taking place on the last word of the verse. Notice, too, that each verse (except the final) ends on the dominant-seventh chord (G_7). Don't begin playing the tonic chord (in this case, C) in subsequent verses until you begin to sing. <u>This is very important.</u>

You know, you have to be comfortable singing these songs as well as playing them. If "Frankie..." was too high for you in C try it in A.

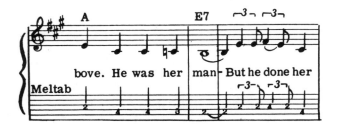

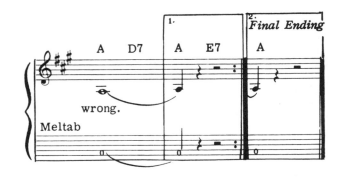

Play the melody

The reason for writing out the song twice in two different keys was not merely to save you the trouble of transposing a simple song. A very important point must be made here - at the outset of study. A great many factors combine to make a blues guitarist out of "just a" guitarist. It would be difficult to single out any one facet of the art as the most important. However, the sine quo non of the blues guitarist is the ability to play the melody of any of the songs he sings. That's our axiom for today. It's worthy of being put in a box.

> *If a blues guitarist you would be,*
> *Learn to play the melody! (anon.)*

Writing out the melody in two keys will serve as a guide for the playing of same. Try it an octave higher than written. Try it in still another key or two... When the time will come (very soon) to begin creating your own bluesy instrumental passages and solos you will find that the inspiration for them will spring largely from the very tune of the song being played. And, of course, your sheer technical facility in getting around the fingerboard will have been greatly strengthened.

Returning to our basic strum once again here is one of the oldest blues known in the characteristic three-line form:

JOE TURNER

Guitar Rhythm

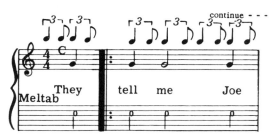

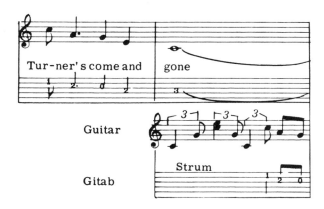

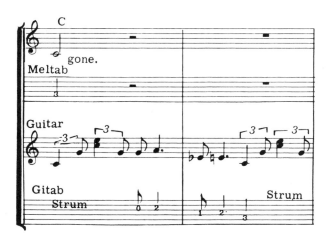

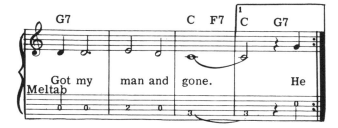

Final Ending

He come with forty links of chain.
He come with forty links of chain (Oh, Lordy)
Got my man and gone.

They tell me Joe Turner's come and gone,
They tell me Joe Turner's come and gone...
Done left me here to sing this song.

Come like he never come before.
Come like he never come before...
Got my man and gone.

11

Note the characteristic break[1] in measures three, seven and eight. This time let's try it a little higher – in E.

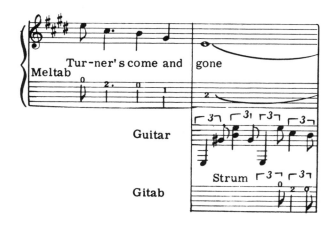

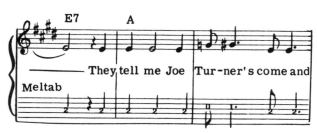

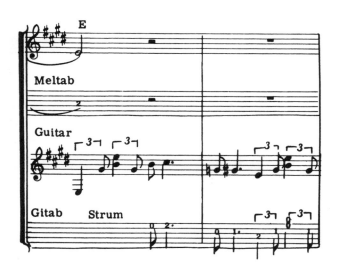

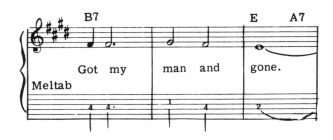

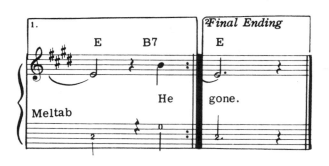

Concluding Passages

A very important place in the song to begin building is at the very end. While singing the last word, "gone..." play this descending series of diminished chords.

In C:

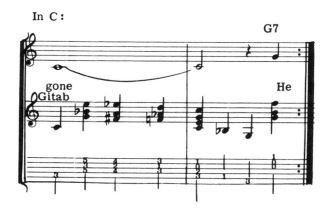

In E:

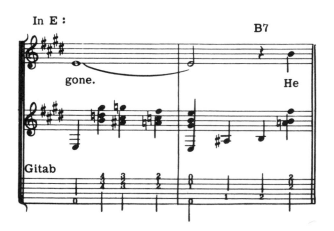

[1] More on this later beginning on page 54

You can vary the rhythm and contour of this passage in any number of ways:

Be sure to keep singing "gone..." as you play these chords.

You can do similar things in "Frankie and Johnny" on the last word, "wrong".

These concluding passages may also be used as introductions of a kind.

Remember: If used as an introduction or conclusion for all verses except the last, these passages end on the dominant-seventh chord. In the final verse the phrase comes to rest on the tonic chord on the fifth beat of the passage.

Just to round out the picture a bit more here's "Careless Love" with some extra chords thrown in which may not have occured to you.

CARELESS LOVE

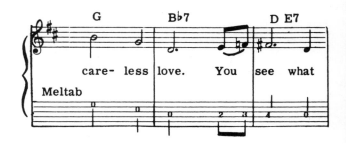

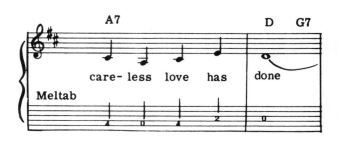

Play this when singing the last word of each verse except the final. In the final verse play only the first five chords of the sequence.

I cried last night and the night before (3x)
Gonna cry tonight and cry no more.

I love my momma and my poppa too (3x)
But I'd leave them both to go with you.

When I wore my apron low (3x)
You'd follow me through rain and snow.

Now I wear my apron high (3x)
You see my door and pass right by.

Love, oh, love...

14

ANOTHER BLUES STRUM

Finger an E chord.

Part 1

The thumb strikes the sixth string and then brushes rapidly downward across the rest of the strings. As the thumb moves across the strings, the wrist, which is normally arched, is lowered until the heel of the hand is brought into contact with the vibrating strings, thereby muffling them. The rhythmic figure produced by this part of the strum is

Part 2

At the beginning of the second half of this pattern, the right hand which has moved vertically downward across the strings, now moves rapidly upward as the first finger brushes over the strings (highest note first; lowest, last). Then, either the thumb or the finger nails are brought rapidly downward over the strings again with the same muffling motion of the wrist. This completes the cycle

and we are ready to begin again.

The whole pattern looks like this:

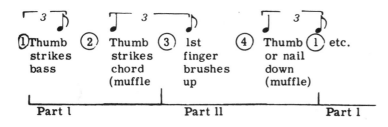

If you're not sure what the rhythm sounds like, sing (to yourself) The Worms Crawl In, The Worms Crawl Out:

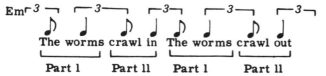

Better - listen to Josh White sing almost any of his blues.... Like Number 12 Train.

Let's try "Number Twelve Train" in the key of E. It may be a bit high for you to sing in this key but most guitarists favor E for playing blues. Some of the reasons for the advantages of playing in E will become apparent in this song.

NUMBER TWELVE TRAIN

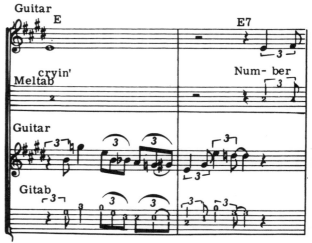

16

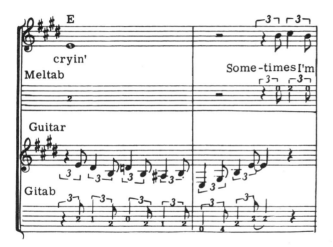

She left me all night long, I could not help
    myself (2x)
I thought she was loving me, I found she was
    loving somebody else.

I may be wrong, but I'll be right some day (2x)
But the next gal I get will have to do what poppa
    say.

Your first full-fledged breaks appear at the end
of the first and second phrases of the melody and the
familiar descending series of diminished chords is
heard at the end.

17

When Josh plays this song he employs a lengthy introduction with all kinds of typical blues devices. Here is a transcription of that intro as well as as analysis of it as they appear in my Thesis:

The overall effect produced by this instrumental introduction is that of a train starting, gradually picking up speed, getting faster and faster, blowing its whistle, and finally slowing down to a halt before the voice enters. This is accomplished by a series of ingenious musical devices and sound effects.

We have the first one in the initial measure. At some indeterminate position up the neck of the guitar, the E string and the A string are fingered in a double stop. The two strings are struck sharply by the right hand. At the instant of striking, the double stop is slid very rapidly down the neck of the instrument, breaking off, again, at some (lower) indeterminate position. The quality of tone thus produced is an explosive one, not unlike the first burst of steam issuing from a starting locomotive.

A series of slow, very staccato E major chords then begins. The palm of the right hand is brought down over the strings, muffling them almost immediately after their having been struck, thus producing the desired effect of the slowly moving train... In the third measure, eighth notes take the place of quarters as the train begins to pick up speed. Measures four to seven are repeated, getting faster and faster, with the pulse now coming every second beat instead of every fourth. (There is no actual "repeat" in the strict musical sense. White merely plays a passage of nine identical measures of $\frac{2}{4}$ - identical except for the steady _accelerando_. To save space this was written in our example as a repeat.)

At measure ten, $\frac{4}{4}$ returns - and in a most interesting and beautiful manner. The heavy accented chords give way to a steady flow of single eighth notes on the E* string (played with the thumb), over which may be heard a series of "train whistle" double stops, played on the first and second (e' and b)* strings with the first two fingers. This is a delicate problem in manual coordination and White handles it flawlessly.

The whistle effect is obtained first, by sliding g'-natural (third fret, e' string) and e'-flat (fourth fret, b string) up one fret each to g'-sharp and e'-natural. A more unusual quality is produced, in measures eleven and twelve, when the notes are slid down instead of up.

At measure thirteen, the heavily accented chords return as the train begins to slow down. At measure sixteen the opening "explosion" is repeated.

This, to all intents and purposes, ends the introduction even though there is one more measure of instrumental playing before the voice enters. In this last measure (seventeen), the actual accompaniment figure makes its first appearance...

As you can see and hear, this is rather complicated guitaring. Don't feel you have to master this (or any other example herein contained) at once. Playing the blues is a lifetime affair and blues guitarists are usually accomplished specialists.

---

* This letter notation system used by musicologists gives the actual pitch of the note. In this system the strings of the guitar are written E A d g b e'.

18

Please note that unlike the first basic blues strum you learned - and probably most of the other guitar strums you know- the first beat if this "Josh White strum" does not get the accent even though it consists of the thumb playing the bass note of the chord. Rather, the accent falls on the second beat (the strum down across the whole chord). This produces an interesting counter rhythm between the actual pulse of the strum and the changing of the chords. Since blues chords generally change at regular intervals and usually on the first (or third) beat of a measure this strum produces a conflict because it begins one eighth-note (actually one "triplet eighth-note") before the first (and third) beats of each measure.

That means that even though the chord symbols will continue to be written in their customary places (over beats one and three) when using this strum you will have to anticipate the changes by that preliminary, unaccented thumb-on-the-bass-note part of the strum. Saying it another way for the scientists in the audience: The melody and the chord changes are slightly out of phase with each other. For the sake of clarity, in this example the chord changes are written where they actually occur.

19

St. James Infirmary

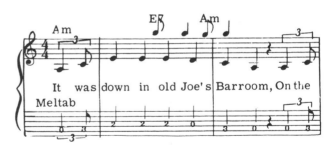

It was down in old Joe's Barroom, On the

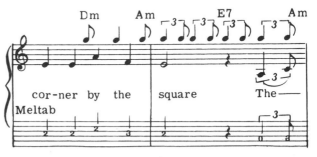

cor-ner by the square The —

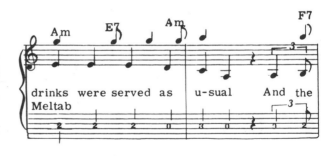

drinks were served as u-sual And the

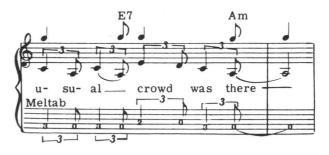

u- su- al — crowd was there —

On my left stood big Joe McKennedy,
His eyes were bloodshot red.
He turned to the crowd around him,
These were the very words he said.

"I went down to the St. James Infirmary
"To see my baby there.
"She was stretched out on a long white table,
"So pale, so cold and so fair."

Chorus

Let her go, let her go, God bless her,
Wherever she may be.
She may search this whole world over,
Never find a man as sweet as me.

When I die, please bury me
In my high-top Stetson hat.
Put a twenty-dollar gold piece on my watch
           chain,
So the gang'll know I died standing pat.

I want six crap shooters for pall bearers.
Six pretty gals to sing me a song.
Put a jazz band on my hearse wagon
To raise hell as we stroll along.

And now that you've heard me story,
I'll have another shot of booze.
And if anybody happens to ask you,
I've got the St. James Infirmary blues.

Chorus

CHOKING THE STRINGS

Learning to play blues guitar is a cumulative process although not necessarily a graded one. It is difficult to present material in a smooth ascending curve of levels of difficulty. For example, there is the relatively simple device known as pulling or choking the strings which under certain conditions produces the bluesiest of all blues sounds.

In A minor attack the third fret of the second string as follows:

Press down normally with the third or fourth finger and play that note (d). Then, keeping the finger in firm contact with the fret pull the string downward or upward as shown in the diagram while the original note is still sounding. The pitch will rise approximately half a tone. Then allow the string to return to its original position and the note will return to d.

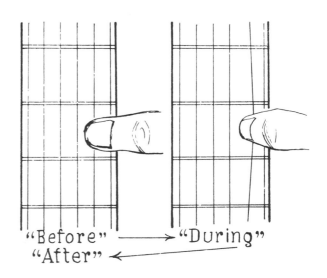

"Before" ⟶ "During"
"After" ⟵

Here are some examples of choking the strings in the songs already taken up.

You will observe that the "choked" notes involve either the flatted third, fifth or seventh of the chord being played. These notes are known as "blue notes".

St. James Infirmary

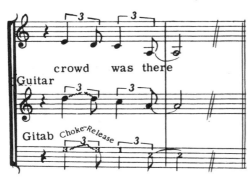

Frankie & Johnny (1)

Frankie & Johnny (11)

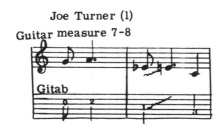

Joe Turner (1)
Guitar measure 7-8

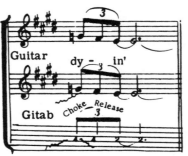

Joe Turner (11)

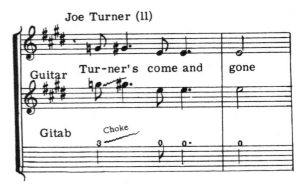

Carless Love
(variant)

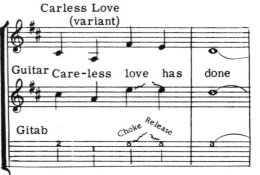

Number 12 Train

22

WALKING BASS AND BOOGIE WOOGIE

In its simplest form the boogie-woogie walking bass consists merely of playing the notes of a chord one at a time with the addition of either the sixth or the flatted seventh of the scale to the basic first, third and fifth notes of the chord.

23

In actual practice the guitarist usually alternates each down stroke on the bass with an up stroke on the chord. This up stroke may either be played with the first finger brushing over the strings in an upward direction or with the fingers plucking the first three strings in the normal manner.

Do the same thing with the other chords illustrated above. When the "bass" gets up into the treble strings you may have only two or one strings to pluck. Adjust your right hand accordingly.

When these patterns are used to accompany a song they produce a wonderful, driving effect as a complement to the voice. Here's the way Leadbelly played "Good Morning, Blues":

GOOD MORNING BLUES

①

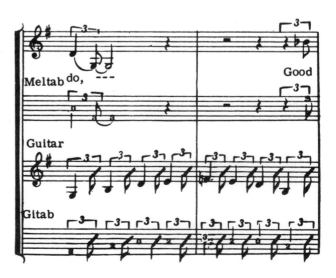

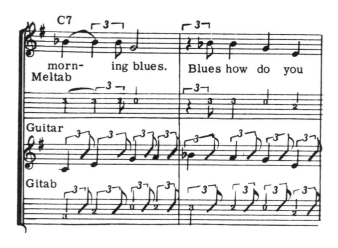

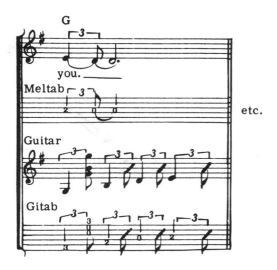

etc.

I lay down last night, turning from side to side (2x)
I was not sick, I was just dissatisfied.

I woke up this morning, blues walking 'round my bed (2x)
Went to eat my breakfast the blues were all in my bread.

I sent for you yesterday, here you come a-walking today (2x)
You got your mouth wide open, you don't know what to say.

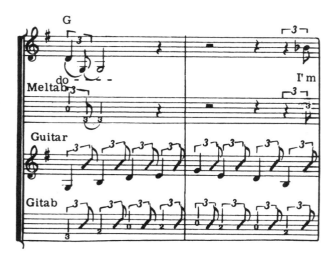

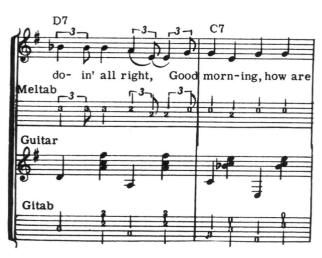

25

Try the same song in E♭

Good Morning Blues (II)

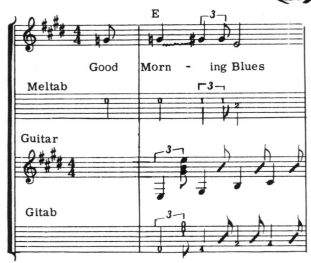

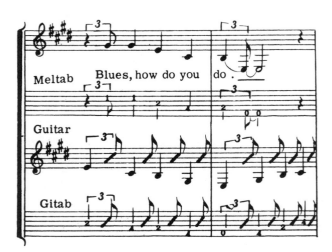

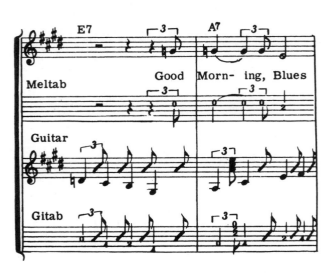

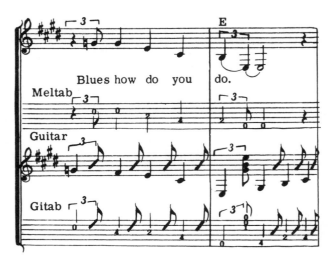

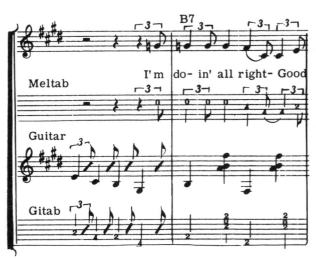

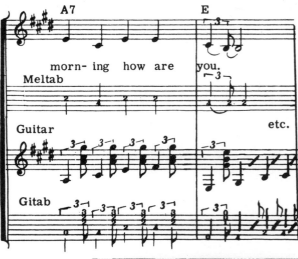

26

GET THEE BEHIND ME, SATAN (I)

Here's one the Almanacs used to sing:

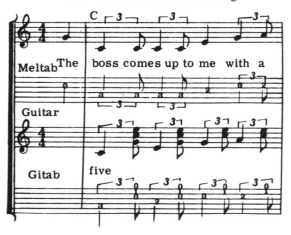

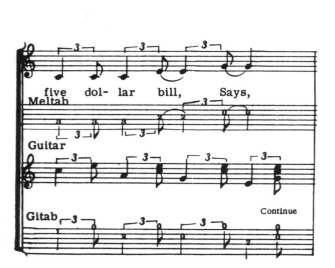

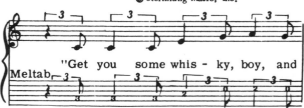

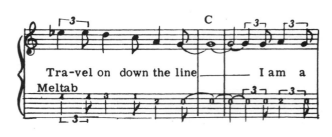

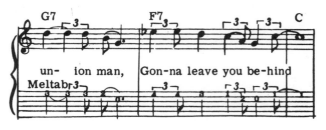

Get Thee Behind Me, Satan (II)

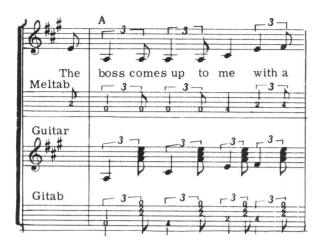

The boss comes up to me with a

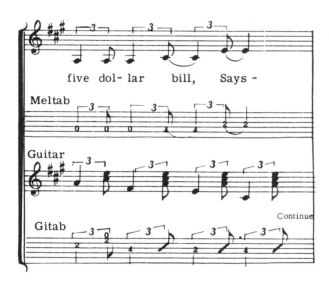

five dol-lar bill, Says -

"Get you some whis-ky, boy, and

drink your fill. "Get thee be-hind me, Sa-tan,

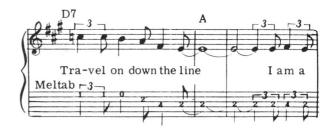

Tra-vel on down the line   I am a

un-ion man,   Gon-na leave you be-hind.

Redheaded woman took me out to dine,
Said, "Love me baby, leave your union behind."

Chorus
On the Fourth of July the politicians say,
"Vote for us and we'll raise your pay."

Chorus

Company union sent out a call,
"Join us in the summer, we'll forget you in the
fall."

Chorus

If anyone should ask you your union to sell,
Just tell 'em where to go **and send 'em back to
hell.**

Chorus

29

And finally, "The Midnight Special"...

The Midnight Special (I)

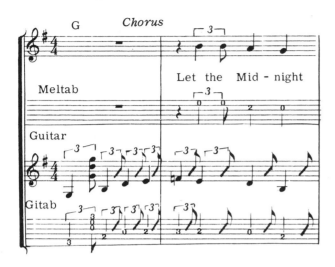

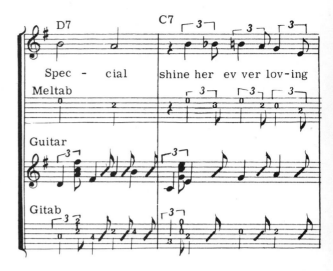

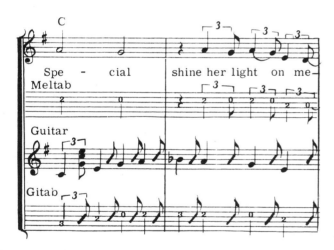

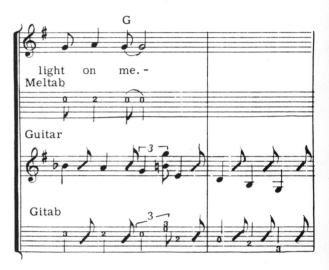

Well, you wake up in the morning,
Hear the ding-dong ring.
You go a-marching to the table,
See the same damn' thing.

Well, it's on a-one table,
Knife and fork and a pan.
And if you say anything about it,
You're in trouble with the man.

Chorus

If you ever go to Houston,
Man, you better walk right.
And you better not stagger
And you better not fight.

Sheriff Benson will arrest you,
And he'll carry you down.
And you can bet your bottom dollar,
Penitentiary bound.

Chorus

Yonder comes Miss Rosie,
Tell me how do you know?
I know her by her apron,
And the dress she wore.

Umbrella on her shoulder,
Piece of paper in her hand,
Well, I heard her tell the captain,
"I want my man."

Chorus

I'm goin' away to leave you,
And my time it ain't long.
The man is gonna call me,
And I'm goin' home.

Then I'll be done all my grievin'
Whoopin', hollerin' and cryin';
Then I'll be done all my studyin'
'Bout my great long time.

Chorus

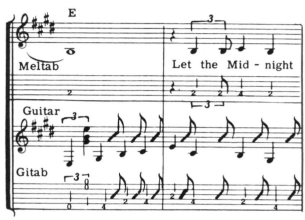

THE MIDNIGHT SPECIAL (II)

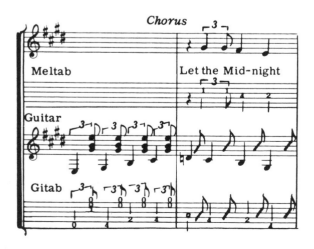

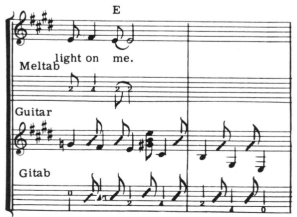

THE FLAT PICK AND THE CHURCH LICK

A great deal of good blues music can be made with a flat pick. Particularly in the realm of white blues - that is, hillbilly and cowboy derived melodies, yodels and rhythms coupled with Negro blues harmonies. Use of the pick is limited almost strictly to steel-string guitars - nylon strung instruments just don't respond well to the pick.

The pick should not be too stiff.

With the pick grasped firmly but flexibly between the thumb and the forefinger just try strumming a few chords in a simple bass-chord pattern. Try alternating basses. You may run into difficulty hitting the string you want to until you get used to the feel of the pick. That shouldn't take too long. Don't bang the strings too hard - that's not the purpose of using a pick.

A good rhythmic feeling is achieved when you strike the chord lightly on the way up as well as on the way down. Woody Guthrie used to call it the "church lick" and he used it to play many of the songs in his vast repertoire of folksongs and original compositions.

Play an E chord.

Pick the bass string - then all the rest downward. Then come back up over the first three or four strings.

Down, Down, Up

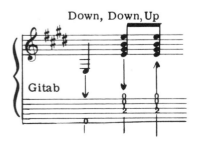

Gitab

THE CHURCH LICK WITH THE BLUES WRINKLE

Many of the songs of Woody Guthrie, the Carter Family, Jimmie Rodgers and others have blues feeling (if they are not actually blues) and sound particularly well when played with this strum.

Finger an E major chord and play "bass-down bass-up-down-up" in the following rhythmic pattern:

count: Bass down Bass up down up
        1   2   3- and   4- and

Make sure that the "and" after "3" is an upstroke.

After you get this pattern running smoothly try lifting the first finger (left hand) off the G string on "4" and putting it back on the following "and".

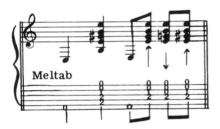

Meltab

On the A chord you'll have to revise your fingering a bit to get this blues wrinkle to sound.

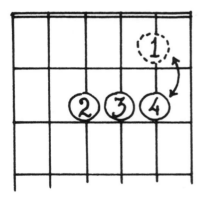

Keep your first finger on the first fret of the B string and lift the pinky off on "4" and replace it on "and".

Meltab

32

Now let's try <u>Mule Skinner Blues</u>...

MULE SKINNER BLUES

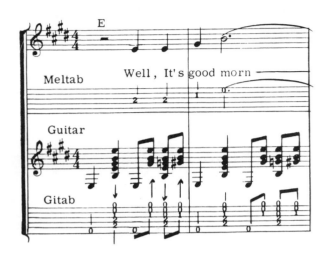

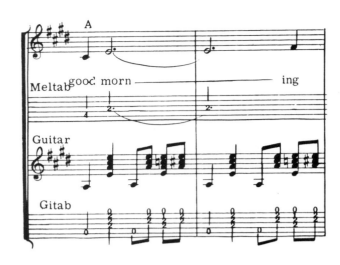

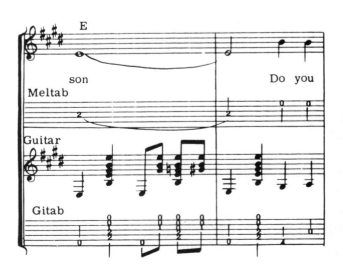

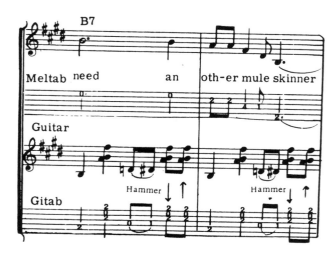

Meltab: need an oth-er mule skinner

Guitar

Hammer

Gitab

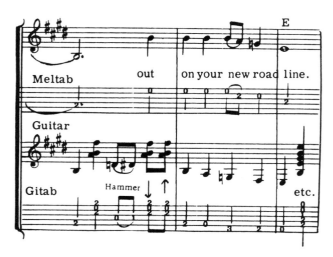

Meltab: out on your new road line.

Guitar

Hammer

Gitab: etc.

Well, I like to work - I'm rolling all the time,
Yes, I like to work - I'm rolling all the time.
I can pop my initials right on the mule's behind.

Well it"'s, Hey, little water boy, bring your
water 'round
Hey, little water boy, bring your water "round.
If you don't like your job set that water bucket
down.

I'm a-working on the new road at a dollar and
a dime a day.
Working on that new road at a dollar and a
dime a day.
I got three women waiting on a Saturday night
just to draw my pay.

Use the same strum with me.

Marryin' Blue Yodel

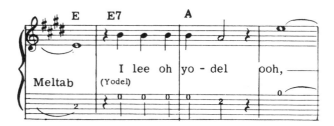

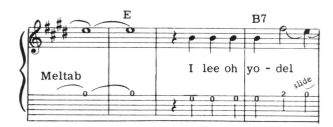

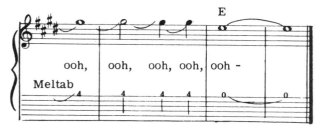

Well, it's T for Texas, T for Tennessee (2x)
And it's T for Thelma - the gal who made a
fool out of me.

If you don't like me, Thelma, you don't have to
stall (2x)
'Cause I can get me more women than a passen-
ger train can haul.

I'm gonna but me a shotgun, long as I am tall
(2x)
Gonna shoot old Thelma - just to see her
jump and fall.

I'd like to be your sidetrack, baby, till your
mainline comes (2x)
I can do more switchin' than your mainline ever
done.

(Optional yodel after every verse)

I was a stranger passing through your town (2x)
When I asked for a favor, good gal, you done
turned me down.

I'd rather drink muddy water and sleep in a
hollow log (2x)
Than stay here in Houston, good gal, and be
your salty dog.

You may see me talking - walking down the
railroad track (2x)
But, good gal, you done me wrong and I ain't
never comin' back.

I rode the southern, I rode the L. and M. (2x)
And if the railroad cops don't get me, I'll ride
on them again.

I like Mississippi, I'm a fool about Tennessee
(2x)
But these Oklahoma women 'bout got the best
of me.

What makes the rooster crow at the break of
day? (2x)
To let the little dog know that the big dog is on
his way.

37

THE PERIPATETIC PINKY

A much-neglected finger is the pinky of the left hand. It's usually the last finger to be used in a chord and most of the time it just hangs there patiently. It is precisely for that reason that using the pinky in certain situations will add a delightful sparkle to an otherwise complete strum and chord situation.

Let's develop an interesting _pick_ and pinky pattern.

First, the rhythm.

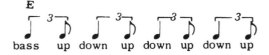

bass   up   down   up   down   up   down   up

Now add the pinky on the 2nd, 3rd and 4th beats playing c#, d and c#, respectively.

Try a similar pattern with an A chord. Depending on how you finger A you may use the third and/or the fourth finger:

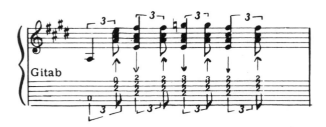

Play A as a barre chord on the fifth fret and add the pinky in precisely the same way you did with the initial E chord.

Do the same thing with B at the seventh fret.

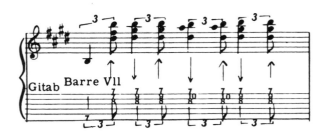

Now try B as a barre chord on the second fret. This is analogous to the first A chord pattern. See page 40 for the proper fingering.

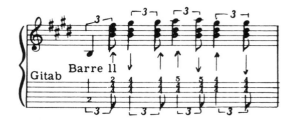

Here is the same series of chords with a slight variation of the pinky.

Can you spot it?

38

Now dig this:

LONG·LINE SKINNER

Adapted by Jerry Silverman

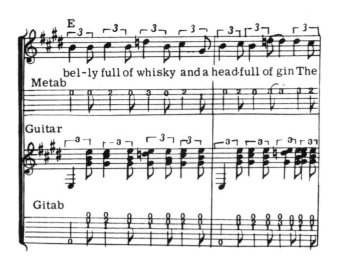

40

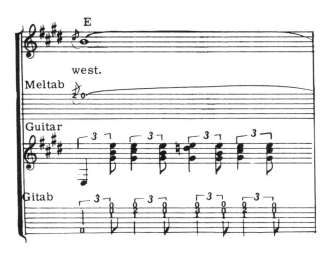

west.

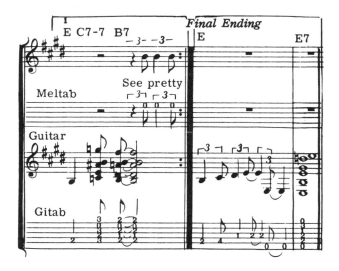

Final Ending

See pretty

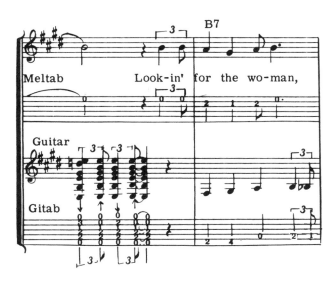

Look-in' for the wo-man,

See, pretty mama, pretty mama, see what you
    done done;
You made your daddy love you, now your man
    done come.

Chorus

I'm down in the bottom skinning mules for
    Johnny Ryan;
A puttin' my initials on a mule's behind.

Chorus

When the weather it gets chilly gonna pack up
    my line,
'Cause I ain't skinning mules in the winter
    time.
                      Chorus

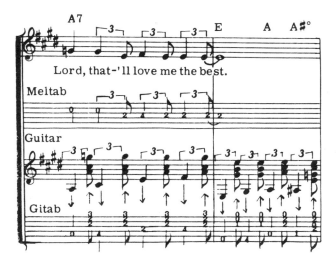

Lord, that-'ll love me the best.

THE "SEVEN-SEVENTH" CHORD

Mention must be made here of an extremely important blues chord

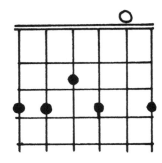

Physically, as you can see, it is nothing more than a B7th chord moved up one fret to C7th. It is played with the dissonant addition of the open B string. Actually, in context the open B string is not really added but rather left over or "suspended" from the E chord which usually preceeds it and becomes consonant (more or less) in the B7th chord which usually follows it.

Functionally, it serves as a leading (or dominant) chord to the B7th at the end of a verse just prior to the return to the tonic chord of the next verse.

In order to identify this chord in the customary shorthand-symbol manner and since it is made up of the notes C, E, G, Bflat and B (the latter two notes being a minor seventh and a major seventh above C, (respectively) we shall call it C7-7th (read, C seven-seventh).

Some other of these "seven-seventh" chords conveniently played are:

B♭7-7th-A7-D.   E♭7-7th-D7-G.   F7-7th-E7-A.

These other chords do not have exactly the same relationship of chord tone to open string dissonance as C7-7th but we may as well use the same generic name for them.

Let's take a quick look back at some of the songs already covered and see where we can play these chords:

Frankie and Johnny

But he done her wrong.

Careless Love

Care-less love has done

Number Twelve Train

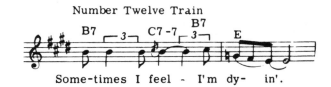

Some-times I feel - I'm dy- in'.

St. James Infirmary

Crowd was there.

Good Morning Blues (1)

Morn-ing how are you ——

Good Morning Blues (11)

B7   C7-7 B7   E

Morn-ing how are you. ——

42

Get Thee Behind Me Satan (11)

Gon - na leave you — be - hind

Midnight Special (I)

Light on me

Midnight Special (11)

Light on me —

Long Line Skinner

Lord that'll love me the best

FINGER-PICKING AND THE INDEPENDENT THUMB

The old adage about the right hand not knowing what the left hand is doing is doubly true of the guitar. Not only must the actions of both hands be separated (albeit coordinated) but the fingers of the right hand must be trained to move "independently" of each other. Particularly must the thumb be able to keep a steady, "square" beat in the bass while various combinations of the fingers go to town on the upper strings.

Finger an E chord.

Get the thumb going slowly and steadily on the bass string. (The thumb may strike more than one string at a time or alternate basses.)

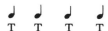

Pluck the first string simultaneously with the bass. Use your first and second fingers alternately on the first string.

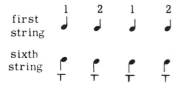

Pluck the first string twice as fast as the bass. Maintain the attention of the first and second fingers.

Now pluck the first string using the blues trochaic rhythm of the very first strum illustrated in this book.

Leave out the first, seventh and eighth strokes on the first string but continue the bass as before.

43

After you feel comfortable with this syncopation try playing different notes on the upper strings.

Now go exploring. Fourth fret, fifth fret, sixth... sev...

If you can manage to mash your third finger down over the fourth, third and second strings without covering the first while playing that barre you'll be able to play the same pattern you did with the open A chord. This one isn't easy. Practice, practice, practice!

Using this barre chord position at any fret get the pinky moving in a similar pattern. For example, at the third fret the chord would be G. Reach with the pinky to the sixth fret (b-flat).

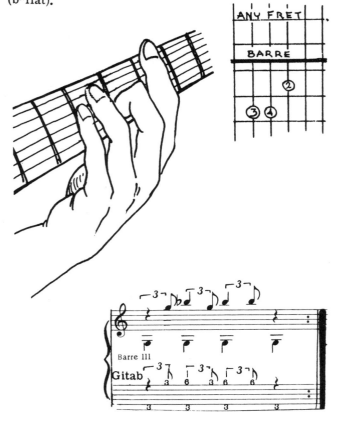

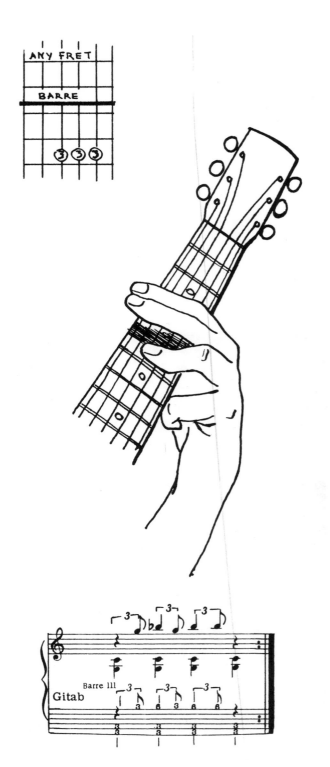

44

Darlin'

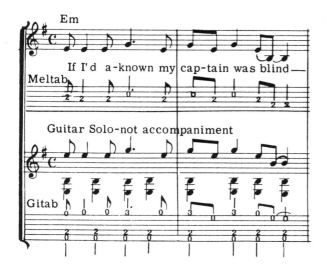

SPORTIN' LIFE BLUES

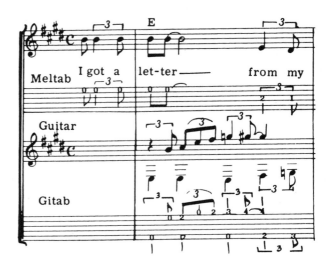

Asked my captain for the time of day, darlin',
    darlin' (2)
Asked my captain for the time of day,
He got so made he threw his watch away, darlin',
    darlin'.

Fight my captain and I'll land in jail, darlin',
    darlin', (2)
Fight my captain and I'll land in jail,
Nobady 'round to go my bail, darlin', darlin'.

If I'd a-had my weight in lime, darlin', darlin',
    (2)
If I'd a-had my weight in lime,
I'd have whipped that captain till he went stone
    blind, darlin', darlin'.

If I'd a-listened to what my mama said, darlin',
    darlin', (2)
If I'd a-listened to what my mama said,
I'd be at home and in my mama's bed, darlin',
    darlin'.

Repeat verse one

46

Sport- in' life is kil — lin' me —

1.
My moth-er

2.

My mother used to say to me,
So young and foolish, that I can't see.
Ain't got no mother, my sister and brother won't
    talk to me.

I've been a liar and a cheater too,
Spent all my money on booze and you.
That old night life, that sportin' life is killin'
    me.

My mother used to say to me,
So young and foolish, that I can't see.
Ho, Jerry, hey there Jerry, why don't you
    change your ways?

I've been a gambler and a cheater too,
But now it's come my turn to lose,
That old sportin' life has got the best hand,
    what can I do?

There ain't but one thing that I've done wrong,
Lived this sportin' life, my friend, too long;
I say it's no good, please believe me, please
    leave it alone.

I'm gettin' tired of runnin' 'round,
Think I will marry and settle down;
That old night life, that sportin' life is killin'
    me.

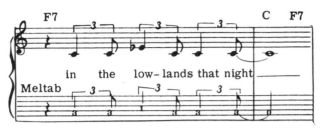

THE BREAK

One of the major characteristics of blues melodies is the pause in the vocal part between phrases. If the stanza is three lines long, consisting of twelve measure of music, the chances are that only approximately six of those measures will be vocalized. The pauses in the singing generally occur two measures at a time at the end of the first, second and third lines, respectively.

BACKWATER BLUES

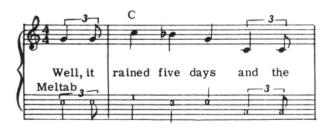

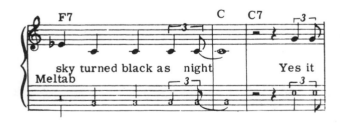

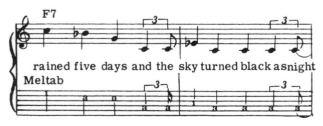

Well, It thundered and it lightened and the winds began
to blow (2x)
There was thousands of people didn't have no place to
go.

I woke up this morning, couldn't even get out my
door (2x)
Enough trouble to make a poor boy wonder where he
gonna go.

I went out to the lonesome, high old lonesome hill (2x)
And looked down on the old house where I used to
live.

Backwater blues have caused me to pack up my things
and go (2x)
'Cause my house fell down and I can't live there no
more.

48

When the voice is singing the guitar may content itself with "merely" playing the accompaniment. But in those pauses - those breaks - it is virtually incumbent upon the guitarist to fill in with meaningful instrumental passages or, as they are called, "breaks". We've been introducing some breaks here and there into the material already covered but we have not as yet gone into any detail as to the how and why of them.

This "how and why" is the backbone of the blues guitar for you will note that in any typical blues verse the guitar must solo roughly 50% of the time!

In this typical three-line, three-break verse of ours the following chord pattern is the most commonplace:

The concluding break of any verse may be used as an introduction to the first verse. The last chord of the intro must always be the dominant-seventh (V_7) which will then lead into the tonic (I) of the first line.

When playing a break keep your fingers on or near the indicated chord whenever possible.

The break serves a dual function.

(1) As a filler during moments of vocal rest.

(2) As an harmonic and melodic bridge between the chords on either side of it. It follows from this that the breaks listed as "I", "II", "III" in the previous musical example should be somewhat different in harmonic and melodic makeup since they link different pairs of chords. There is, of course, a unity in this duality.

Very often, as has been stated before, the inspiration for these breaks comes from the melody of the song. However, as there is a basic similarity in most blues melodies, certain instrumental passages do recur often enough for them to be thought of as "standard". This standardization is thought of not in terms of the actual notes of the breaks themselves but in their general contour.

49

For reference, practice, use and as models for
your own original breaks the following 75 examples
of breaks are presented in the five common folk-blues
guitar keys.

Try fitting some breaks into Backwater Blues.
And other blues.

75 BREAKS- A BONANZA!

C Major - Break III

G Major - Break I

G Major- Break ll

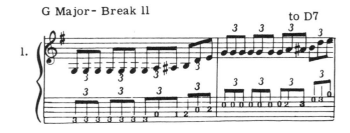

G Major - Break lll

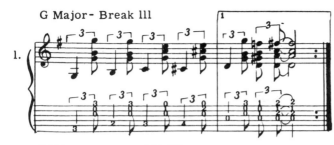

1.

² Final Ending

2.

Final Ending

3.

Final End.

4.

Barre lll

5.

1.   **Final End.**

D Major - Break l

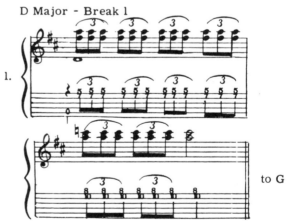

1.

to G

2.

53

D Major - Break 11

to
A7

D Major -Break
111

1.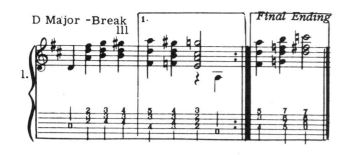

2.

3.

4.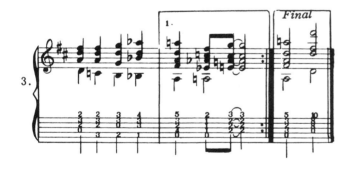

5.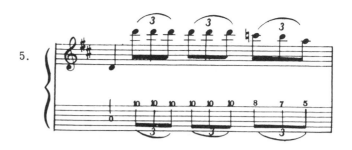

55

A Major - Break I

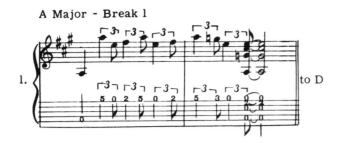

1. to D

2.

3. Barre V

4.

5.

A Major - Break II

1. to E7

2.

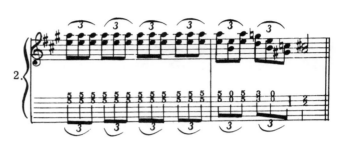

3. E7

4.

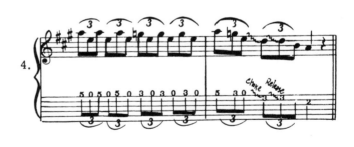

5,

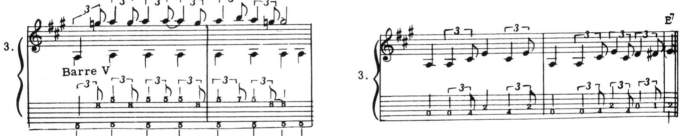

56

A Major - Break lll

4.

Barre V

Final Ending

1.

1.

Final Ending

2.

Final End.

3.

Final End

5.

1.

Final Ending

E Major - Break 1

1.

To A

2.

slide

E Major - Break 11

1. to B7

3.

3.

4.

4.

5.

5.

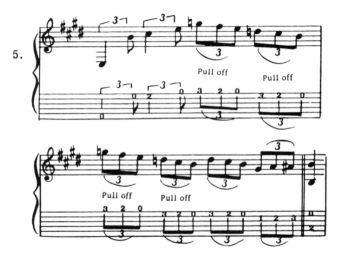

E Major-Break III

59

Here are 5 blues presented <u>sans</u> breaks.   Go to it!

Long Handled Shovel

by Jerry Silverman

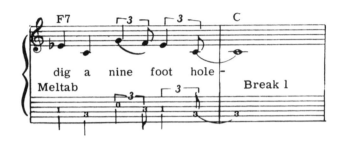

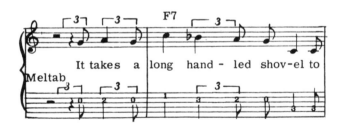

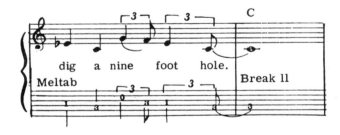

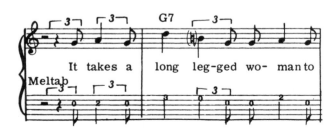

It takes a two-bladed ax, Lord, to cut this timber
    down (2x)
It takes a two-timin' woman to make me leave this
    town.

It takes a fast-movin' rattler to take me from this
    place (2x)
It takes a fast-talkin' mama to laugh right in my face.

It takes a six-string guitar to help me sing this song
    (2x)
It takes a six-shot pistol - and I'll be long time gone.

New Strangers Blues

I'm a | stranger here, | Just blowed into
Meltab

town. | I'm a | stran-ger here,
Meltab Break(1)

just blowed in-to | town.
Meltab | Break ll

Just be- | cause I'm a stran-ger ev-'ry
Meltab

bo-dy wants to dog me 'round. | Break lll
Meltab

Lord, I wonder do my good gal know I'm here (2x)
Well, if she do, she sure don't seem to care.

I wonder how some people can dog a poor stranger so
    (2x)
They should remember, they goin' to reap just what
    they sow.

I would stay up North but there's nothing here I can
    do (2x)
But hand around the corner and sing the new
    stranger's blues.

Mama, I am going back South if I wear ninety-nine
    pairs of shoes (2x)
Then I know I'll be welcome and won't have the new
    stranger's blues.

VICKSBURG BLUES

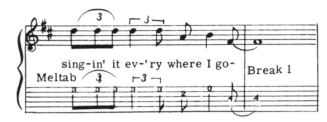

I've got those Vicksburg blues and I'm singing it
    everywhere I please (2x)
Now, the reason I'm singing is to give my poor heart
    some ease.

Now, I don't like this place, mama, and I never will
    (2x)
I can sit right here in jail and look at Vicksburg on
    the hill.

BRICKS IN MY PILLOW

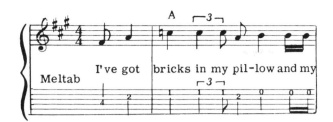

I've got mud in my water, I've got drugs all in my tea (2x)
I've got bugs in my beer, and they keep on biting me.

I've got grounds in my coffee, big boll weevil in my meal (2x)
I've got tacks in my shoes, keep on sticking me in the heel.

I've got holes in my pockets, great big patches on my pants (2x)
I'm behind with my house rent, landlord wants it in advance.

Well, I feel like walking and I feel like lying down (2x)
Well, I feel like drinking, but there ain't no whisky 'round.

When you hear that bell a-ringing and you hear that whistle blow (2x)
Well, I feel like leaving but I don't know where to go.

63

DUST PNEUMONIA BLUES

by Woody Guthrie

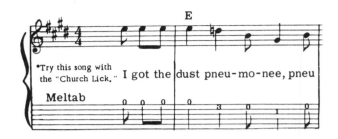

*Try this song with the "Church Lick."

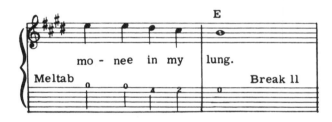

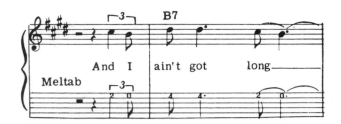

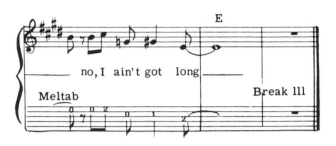

I went to the doctor and the doctor he said "Son" (2x)
"You ain't got long, no, you ain't got long"

My good gal's got the dust pneumonee too (2x)
And she ain't got long, no, she ain't got long.

Down in Texas my good gal fainted in the rain (2x)
I throwed a bucket of dirt in her face and revived her
once again.